Let Freedom Ring

Ulysses S. Grant

by Susan R. Gregson

Consultant:
John Y. Simon, Professor of History
Ulysses S. Grant Association
Southern Illinois University
Carbondale, Illinois

Bridgestone Books
an imprint of Capstone Press
Mankato, Minnesota

Bridgestone Books are published by Capstone Press,
151 Good Counsel Drive • P.O. Box 669 • Mankato, Minnesota 56002.
www.capstonepress.com

Printed in the United States of America

Library of Congress Cataloging-in-Publication Data
Gregson, Susan R.
    Ulysses S. Grant / by Susan R. Gregson.
        p. cm. — (Let freedom ring)
    Includes bibliographical references and index.
    Summary: A biography of the commander of the Union forces in the Civil War who became the eighteenth president of the United States.
    ISBN 0-7368-1091-9 (hardcover)
    ISBN 0-7368-4526-7 (paperback)
    1. Grant, Ulysses S. (Ulysses Simpson), 1822–1885—Juvenile literature.
2. Presidents—United States—Biography—Juvenile literature. 3. Generals—United States—Biography—Juvenile literature. [1. Grant, Ulysses S. (Ulysses Simpson), 1822–1885. 2. Presidents. 3. Generals.] I. Title. II. Series.
E672 .G82 2002
973.8′2′092—dc21   2001004999
                                                                                         CIP

Editorial Credits

Charles Pederson, editor; Kia Bielke, designer and illustrator; Jennifer Schonborn, cover production designer; Deirdre Barton, photo researcher

Photo Credits

CORBIS, cover, 5; Hulton/Archive Photos, 7, 9, 10, 29, 39 (right); Stock Montage, Inc., 13, 23 (left), 31, 35, 43 (bottom); National Portrait Gallery, Washington, D.C./Art Resource, 15, 24, 26, 32, 37, 38, 42, 43; North Wind Picture Archives, 16, 34, 39 (left); David Muench/CORBIS, 21; Unicorn Stock Photos/Batt Johnson, 40

1   2   3   4   5   6   07   06   05   04   03   02

Table of Contents

Chapter One

General and Gentleman

Hiram Ulysses Grant's first name meant "noble one." He shared his middle name with a famous Greek leader who defeated his enemies. Classmates at military school called Ulysses "Sam." On the battlefield, he was sometimes called "U.S.," or "Unconditional Surrender." Some people called him "butcher" because he ordered thousands of men into battle that led to their deaths. Later, people called him "Mr. President."

Ulysses was not a good shopkeeper, farmer, or businessman. He was an average student with a talent for math and painting.

Ulysses, however, found success in the military. He was an outstanding horseman and a fine soldier. During the Mexican War (1846–1848), he was rewarded for his bravery.

Calm and efficient, Ulysses Grant was a strong military leader who helped to end the U.S. Civil War.

In 1861, soldiers of the newly formed Confederacy fired on Northern soldiers at Fort Sumter, South Carolina. The firing of Americans on Americans started the U.S. Civil War (1861–1865).

Ulysses eventually commanded all Northern armies. He defeated Confederate General Robert E. Lee to end the Civil War.

When the war was over, General Grant was elected President Grant. He worked hard to heal the broken nation. But scandals spoiled his second term. Some people he picked for his government were dishonest.

After his presidency, Ulysses lost all his money in bad investments. Once again he seemed to be a failure. Then he developed deadly cancer. He decided to write his memoir, a personal story of the war, before he died. He furiously scribbled as cancer spread throughout his body. Shortly after finishing the book, he died.

Ulysses was known by many names. He will always be remembered as the general who ended a bloody civil war that divided a nation. He helped bring peace and reunite the United States.

Grant's Memoir

The money earned from sales of Ulysses's memoir helped his family after he died. Many people consider his story to be the greatest military memoir ever written.

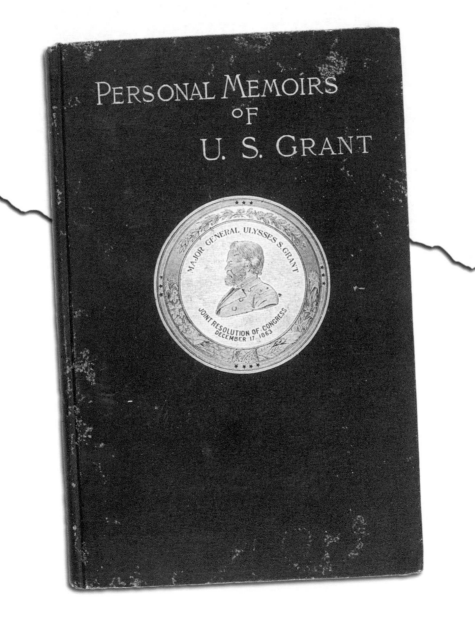

Chapter Two

Growing Up

In his memoir, Ulysses wrote, "I was born on the 27th of April, 1822, at Point Pleasant, Clermont County, Ohio." His father, Jesse, was a farmer and tanner. His mother was named Hannah. By age 7, Ulysses hauled wood for his father's tannery, which turned animal skins into soft leather.

A Gift with Horses

Georgetown, Ohio, where the Grants lived, was a town on the edge of a settled area, or frontier. People had to travel some distance to find a city.

By age 10, Ulysses was known for his talent with horses. Townspeople recommended Ulysses to others who wanted transportation. Soon, young Ulysses was driving customers by horse and wagon up to 40 miles (64 kilometers) away to busier towns.

Ulysses was born in this small house in Ohio. At the time of his birth, Ohio was at the western edge of the United States.

At first, folks thought that letting a boy handle horses was risky. Ulysses, however, proved he had a special touch with these animals. Soon, people brought him horses that were hard to handle. Ulysses was able to calm the horses and get them used to wearing a saddle. This process was called breaking in the horse.

After working here in his father's tannery, Ulysses decided he did not like the work.

Work, Study, and Play

As a boy, Ulysses was trustworthy, hardworking, calm, and determined to finish whatever he started. These traits later shaped Ulysses as a general.

By the time Ulysses was 11, he did an adult's work. He took care of the family farm and its animals. He chopped and hauled wood.

Ulysses had experiences like most children. He found time for basic education in the local school. He also enjoyed swimming, fishing, and ice skating in any spare time he had. And he rode horses whenever he had the chance.

By age 12, Ulysses spent time working in his father's tannery. He worked long enough to decide that he hated the job. He felt most comfortable when he was farming.

In 1838, Jesse applied for Ulysses to go to the United States Military Academy at West Point, New York. Ulysses later said, "A military life had no charms for me, and I had not the faintest idea of staying in the army even if I should be graduated, which I did not expect." Ulysses wanted to be a farmer or a river trader. Jesse Grant insisted.

Off to West Point

Arriving at the academy in 1839, Ulysses learned that he had been enrolled under the wrong name. Instead of "Hiram Ulysses Grant," he was listed as "Ulysses S. Grant." Ulysses did not argue about the mistake. He passed tough entrance exams and began his studies.

Ulysses's classmates called him "Sam," short for "Uncle Sam" after his initials: *U.S.* Students liked him and respected his honesty and fair play. He was an average student, though good at math. Other students thought he was a great horseman. He also painted pictures while at West Point.

From West Point to Missouri

When he arrived at West Point, Ulysses was a farmer. When he left, he was a soldier. He stood tall and upright in his uniform. Ulysses's mother thought he looked like a rugged gentleman.

In 1843, Ulysses graduated as a second lieutenant in the army. He badly wanted to join a cavalry unit so he could ride horses. Instead, he was sent to an infantry, or foot, unit in Missouri.

In Missouri, he met Julia Dent, a classmate's sister. His memoir describes his feelings: "In February she returned to her country home. After that I do not know but my visits became more frequent; they certainly did become more enjoyable." The two became engaged. Before marriage, however, he learned about fighting during the war between Mexico and the United States.

Julia Dent met Ulysses when he served in Missouri. She later married him.

Chapter Three

Going to War

In the 1840s, Mexico and the United States disagreed about the location of the Texas-Mexico border. The U.S. government sent troops to the border, and the Mexican government took this act as a threat. In 1846, Lieutenant Ulysses Grant went to war in Mexico with the Fourth Infantry Regiment of the U.S. Army.

Ulysses proved to be a brave fighter. He distinguished himself time and again through acts of courage. The Mexican War ended in 1848 after the United States captured Mexico City. The United States gained Texas and land that is now New Mexico, Arizona, and California.

Ulysses and his unit returned to Missouri. He and Julia had already become engaged, and they married in the summer of 1848. They later had to live apart when Ulysses was assigned to military posts in Oregon and California.

Young Lieutenant Ulysses Grant fought bravely during the Mexican War.

The Politics of War

Should slavery be extended into new states? The Southern states believed it should be. They did not believe Abraham Lincoln's promises to allow slavery to continue where it already existed.

South Carolina was the first state to secede, or separate, from the Union. The Civil War began in 1861 when Confederate soldiers fired on Fort Sumter, South Carolina. The photo below shows the battered fort after its surrender.

When apart from Julia and a son, recently born Fred, Ulysses was depressed and sometimes drank alcohol. Julia traveled with Ulysses as much as possible to lessen his loneliness. He eventually left the army. His reputation for drinking continued, although he rarely drank in later years.

Soldier to Shopkeeper to Soldier

After leaving the army, Ulysses settled near St. Louis, Missouri. He farmed Julia's family's property and tried several unsuccessful businesses. Times were so bad that one December, he had to sell his watch, probably to buy Christmas gifts.

He moved the family to Galena, Illinois, in 1860. He worked in his father's leather shop, which two of his brothers operated.

Meanwhile, anger between Northern and Southern states was increasing. The North, under Abraham Lincoln, who was elected president in 1860, supported a strong central government. Lincoln opposed extending slavery into newly formed states. However, he promised that slavery could continue in states where it was already legal.

In late 1860, several Southern states left the Union to form their own country, the Confederate States of America. These states wanted the right to keep slaves and did not believe Lincoln's promises.

By 1861, Lincoln was preparing the Union Army for war. He was determined to keep the Union together. Ulysses had rejoined the army and was put in command of a group of volunteers.

Unconditional Surrender

Ulysses and his troops soon earned two victories. They defeated Confederate armies at Fort Henry and Fort Donelson, in Tennessee. These battles were the first major victories for the Union. Until then, the South had dealt its opponents several defeats.

The military leader at Fort Donelson asked for terms before surrendering. Ulysses, however, told them he would accept only their "unconditional surrender." They had to give up without making any demands. Ulysses had earned a new nickname: "unconditional surrender" and was promoted to major general.

The North and South in 1861

When the U.S. Civil War began, 23 Northern states made up the Union. The Confederacy had 11 states.

Chapter Four

General Grant

In 1862, Ulysses nearly lost his next big battle at Shiloh, Tennessee. Confederate soldiers surprised his army while he ate breakfast. It was a tough fight, but the North turned back the South after new Union soldiers arrived. After the Battle of Shiloh, some Union generals grumbled that Ulysses was not worthy of Lincoln's support. The president only said, "I can't spare this man. He fights."

Next, Ulysses set his sights on Vicksburg, Mississippi. Vicksburg was a city in the heart of the South, and Grant wanted to defeat Southern forces there. It was the best way for the North to cut the Southern territory in half.

Vicksburg was surrounded by swamps and the Mississippi River, making it nearly impossible to reach. Heavy cannons protected the city. The swamps stopped the Northern army that fall. Then winter arrived, and Ulysses had to wait for better spring weather before continuing.

Today, the area of the Battle of Vicksburg, Mississippi, is a park (shown above). In 1862 and 1863, Ulysses attacked Vicksburg, a heavily defended city and not easy to defeat.

During May 1863, Ulysses ordered several attacks, but the Southerners stopped them. Finally, Ulysses halted these direct attacks and dug in for a siege. He did not intend to allow any food, people, or weapons into or out of Vicksburg until the city surrendered.

On July 4, 1863, the military commander did surrender. Union forces now controlled the Mississippi River. Lincoln named Ulysses general of the western armies.

After other military actions, Lincoln appointed Ulysses lieutenant general of all the U.S. armies in the war. George Washington had been the last person to hold that position. Only Lincoln himself had more military power than Ulysses.

General in the Trenches

Ulysses was not a picture-perfect general. He often walked around with his uniform unbuttoned. Mud caked his boots. Sometimes, he did not even wear a general's uniform. Instead, he just wore a general's patches on the shoulders of a regular uniform. He almost always had a cigar stuck firmly in his mouth.

People described Ulysses as calm and respectful. He could concentrate for hours on battle plans.

His soldiers loved Ulysses. He rode along the lines on his horse for hours, encouraging his men. He talked often about his family. Documents say that he never told a dirty story or used foul language. In fact, he was known to say only "doggone it" when he was angry.

Ulysses was a popular general. He often rode on horseback and stopped to encourage his soldiers.

Sherman and Grant's Battles

Soon after becoming lieutenant general, Ulysses sent General William T. Sherman to march through Georgia. In 1864, Sherman and his army attacked and destroyed the city of Atlanta. Then they marched to the Atlantic Ocean, winning battle after battle.

Grant went east to find the Virginia forces under Confederate General Robert E. Lee. Ulysses and Lee fought time after time. Ulysses chased Lee through Virginia, losing many battles and thousands of soldiers. The Union Army, however, had many more soldiers than the South did. Ulysses pounded Lee's forces.

General William Sherman led Union troops through the South. His goal was to ruin Southern resources and cut off Confederate troops from each other.

Cold Harbor

At Cold Harbor, Virginia, Ulysses ordered his army to attack a strongly held Southern position. In only an hour, 7,000 Union soldiers and about 2,000 Confederate soldiers were killed or wounded. After the battle, some people in the North called Ulysses "the butcher of Cold Harbor" for sending his soldiers to certain death. He wrote in his memoir, "I have always regretted that the last assault at Cold Harbor was ever made."

Richmond and Petersburg

The South needed to protect Richmond, Virginia, the Confederate capital. The city had strong defenses, and Lee's soldiers continually blocked Ulysses's attacks. Ulysses decided to go around Richmond and attack a town south of there, called Petersburg.

Ulysses's army had lost many more men than Lee's, and Petersburg was strongly defended. However, the North was able to replace its lost soldiers. The South, on the other hand, had few men left to bring into its armies. Ulysses thought it was only a matter of time until the South surrendered.

He laid siege to Petersburg for 10 months. Lee's army tried to escape to join other Confederate forces, but Ulysses's much larger army trapped it.

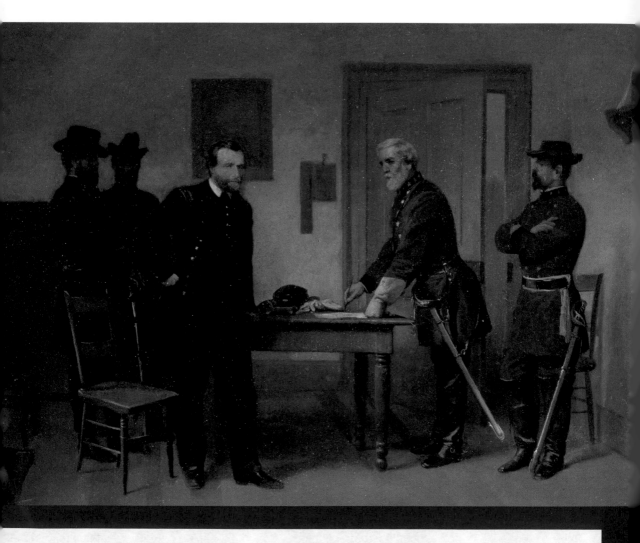

In April 1865, Ulysses (left, leaning on table) accepted the surrender of Robert E. Lee and his armies.

Lee Surrenders

On April 9, 1865, Lee surrendered to Ulysses at Appomattox Court House, Virginia. The two generals talked so easily that Ulysses later said he almost forgot what had brought them to the house.

Ulysses was generous in victory. He allowed Confederate soldiers to keep their personal weapons and horses. Lee was told that his soldiers would not be put in prison but instead could return home. Ulysses gave food to Lee's starving men. These actions were his first steps toward healing the divided nation.

The Appomattox surrender marked the end of the Civil War. Within several weeks, all Confederate troops had given up. Much of the South had been destroyed. Cities and farms were burned. Repairing and constructing buildings would be hard. Rebuilding ruined lives would be harder. Rebuilding a shattered nation would be nearly impossible.

Chapter Five

Mr. President

Five days after Lee surrendered, an angry Southerner named John Wilkes Booth shot and killed President Lincoln. The president and his wife were at a play at Ford's Theatre in Washington, D.C. The president had invited Ulysses and Julia to the play, but they did not attend.

Some historical documents show that Booth and others may have planned to shoot Ulysses the same evening. A man fitting Booth's description had followed the Grants around the city before Lincoln's killing.

Vice President Andrew Johnson became the next president at Lincoln's death. Briefly, in 1867, Ulysses was Johnson's secretary of war. He quit the position when Johnson argued with Congress. Ulysses felt Congress was the voice of the people and should have the last word on decisions.

This book cover shows one artist's idea of how John Wilkes Booth killed Abraham Lincoln.

President Grant

In 1868, Ulysses became the 18th president of the United States. At age 46, Ulysses was the youngest president ever elected. He held that position until John F. Kennedy was elected in 1960 at the age of 43. When Ulysses heard that he was president, he told Julia, "I am afraid I am elected." Ulysses, Julia, and three of their four children moved into the White House.

When Ulysses took over the presidency, America was struggling to recover from the Civil War. Many problems faced his new government. There was the task of rebuilding the South without slave labor. Relations between the federal government and American Indians were tense. The nation had a huge debt to pay. Britain was angry with America. It was a difficult time to be president.

A Tough Job

Ulysses had little experience with government and was uncomfortable being a politician. As president, Ulysses worked on issues he felt would help the

most people. Under his leadership, a
transcontinental railroad was built all the way across
the country. Ulysses also worked to develop a
national park system. His secretary of state

Under Ulysses, the Union Pacific and Central Pacific railroads
finished the transcontinental railroad. Here, the companies, one
working from the East, one from the West, meet in Utah in 1869.

negotiated a peaceful settlement with Britain over warships Britain built for the Confederacy. Ulysses tried to find a peaceful way for the government to work with American Indians.

As president, Ulysses himself was not dishonest. However, he chose assistants who became involved in many scandals.

Ulysses tried to govern as he had led his armies when he was a general. He surrounded himself with people he thought were honest and capable. He then expected them to work together and to share his vision and goals for the country. He was trustworthy and expected the people around him to be trustworthy. But some of them were not, and he had eight difficult years as president.

Second-Term Scandal

By Ulysses's second term as president, it was clear that some of his closest advisers were dishonest. Several officials whom he had appointed were caught cheating the government out of liquor taxes. Others tried to control the gold market to make money. Grant was never accused of being dishonest himself, but he did use bad judgment in appointing officials. He even protected some of his friends from being punished for their actions.

Critics attacked the president for being a weak leader. He admitted his mistakes but kept on as he had when he was a determined youth and general. By the end of his second term, Ulysses was weary and disappointed. He wanted a break.

Around the World

After his presidency ended, Ulysses decided to take an around-the-world trip. It seemed an ideal way to see the world and relax. He, Julia, and their son, 19-year-old Jesse, sailed from Philadelphia in May 1877. Their trip was a complete success. They met kings and queens and were welcomed into the homes of leaders worldwide.

When the Grant family entered San Francisco, huge crowds greeted them enthusiastically.

Guests of Royalty

Here, the Grants bow to Victoria, queen of Great Britain (bowing at left), in London, the British capital city. All over the world, the Grants were popular. World leaders met and welcomed them.

The Grants returned to the United States more than two years and 40 countries later. Thousands of people greeted the Grants when they landed in San Francisco, California, in late 1879. The Grants traveled east to New York City by train. Along the way, people gathered to wave and cheer.

Still popular, Ulysses almost became the Republican candidate for a third term as president. James A. Garfield narrowly defeated him.

Chapter Six

Grant's Gifts to Us

Ulysses and his family decided to settle in New York City in 1884. His son Ulysses Jr. told him about a business firm run by a man named Ferdinand Ward. The former president and his son invested their money and the money of their friends in the new business. Ward then stole the investments.

The former general was left penniless and in debt. He surrendered all of his uniforms, weapons, medals, and gifts from overseas. He literally stripped his walls bare to pay his debts.

Within another six months, Ulysses learned he had throat cancer. Shocked by the news, Ulysses worried that he would die and leave his family with no financial support. The thought was unbearable for a man who believed family was everything.

Ulysses's family, shown here near the end of his life, was important to him. When he learned he had throat cancer, he worried that they might have no money when he died.

Mark Twain

Famous author Samuel Clemens, better known as Mark Twain, was a close friend of Ulysses. Twain urged Ulysses to write a book about his life as soldier and president. He offered Ulysses money to publish the memoir.

Ulysses decided to write a book about his life. In June 1885, friends offered the use of a cottage in the Adirondack Mountains of New York. The Grants lived there while Ulysses continued to write his book. He spent hours bundled in blankets on the front porch, scribbling on a notepad. Visitors gathered at the end of the road, curious to see him at work.

Death Comes to a Warrior

By mid-July, Ulysses had finished the book. He died less than a week later among his family. The book was published and soon earned enough money to support his family.

More than a million people lined New York City's streets for Ulysses's funeral procession. More than 60,000 people marched in the procession. Three U.S. presidents attended the services. Former Confederate and Union officers rode together in the same carriages to honor him. Ulysses was laid in a large tomb. Julia later was buried there, too.

Ulysses finished his memoir at a friend's cottage in New York. Days after he finished writing the book, he died.

A Hero's Achievements

Ulysses's struggle to finish his memoir before dying captures his spirit. As a determined youth and soldier, Ulysses focused on a goal until he achieved it. His life, marked by pain and glory, shows how an ordinary person can do extraordinary things.

As president, Ulysses left the United States with the beginnings of a national park system. He supported the building of a railroad that connected the East and West, making the country stronger. He reduced the national debt and taxes. Ulysses's

Grant's Tomb

Grant's tomb stands on the Upper West Side of Manhattan in New York City. It is the largest burial vault in North America. The words *Let Us Have Peace* are carved on the tomb. Grant used the phrase when he accepted his first nomination for president.

Write a Memoir

Ulysses wrote: "I would like to see truthful history written. Such history will do full credit to the courage, endurance and soldierly ability of the American citizen." His memoir was about the Civil War because it affected his life. Think of a time in your life that affected you and write about it truthfully as your own sort of memoir.

achievements as general of the Union Army, however, far outweigh what he achieved as president.

Ulysses left a stunning memoir of a bitter Civil War. His dedication to the Union ended the bloodiest war in the history of the United States to that time. He knew that the nation must heal. The kindness he felt from all Americans, Northern and Southern, "when it was supposed that each day would prove my last, seemed to me the beginning of the answer to 'Let us have peace.'"

His quiet dignity, honesty, and love of family made Ulysses a good man. His deeds on the battlefield made him a great general. A country that stands united more than a century after his death is Ulysses's gift to the nation.

TIMELINE

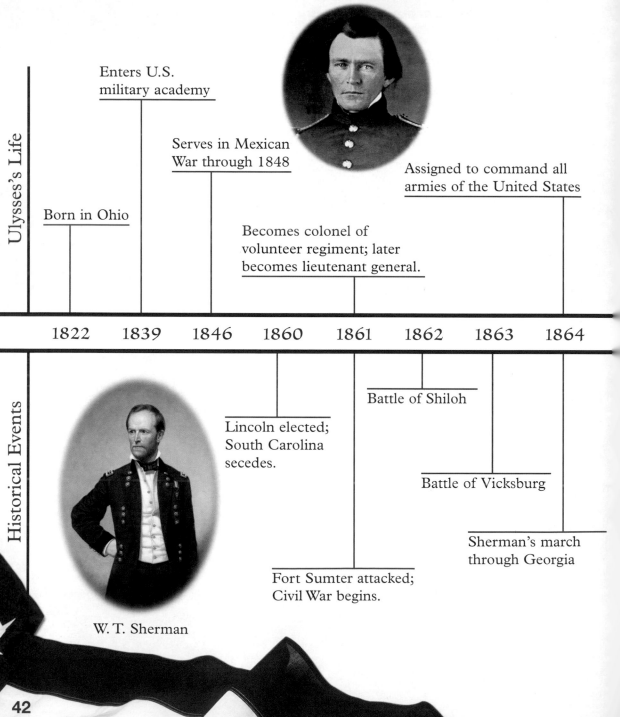

Ulysses's Life

Enters U.S. military academy

Serves in Mexican War through 1848

Assigned to command all armies of the United States

Born in Ohio

Becomes colonel of volunteer regiment; later becomes lieutenant general.

| 1822 | 1839 | 1846 | 1860 | 1861 | 1862 | 1863 | 1864 |

Historical Events

Battle of Shiloh

Lincoln elected; South Carolina secedes.

Battle of Vicksburg

Sherman's march through Georgia

Fort Sumter attacked; Civil War begins.

W. T. Sherman

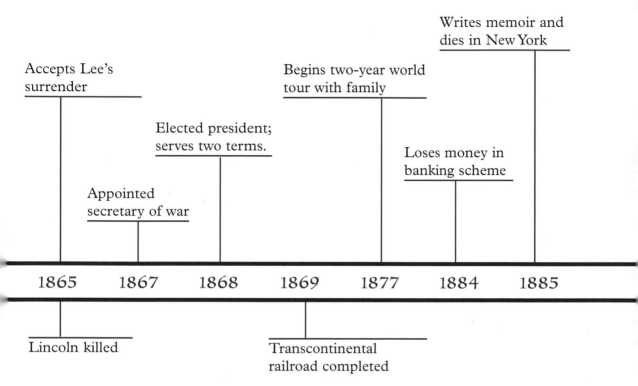

Writes memoir and
dies in New York

Accepts Lee's
surrender

Begins two-year world
tour with family

Elected president;
serves two terms.

Loses money in
banking scheme

Appointed
secretary of war

| 1865 | 1867 | 1868 | 1869 | 1877 | 1884 | 1885 |

Lincoln killed

Transcontinental
railroad completed

Glossary

campaign (kam-PAYN)—series of battles in an area

Confederacy (kuhn-FED-ur-uh-see)—the 11 Southern states that seceded from the United States in 1860 and 1861

frontier (frun-TEER)—area on the edge of a settled region with few people living there

memoir (MEM-wahr)—written remembrance about one's life

secede (si-SEED)—to formally leave an organization

siege (SEEJ)—a long attack that traps defenders within a certain area, such as a city or mountainside

strategy (strah-TUH-gee)—a detailed plan to win a battle, campaign, or war

tactic (TAK-tik)—careful movement used to carry out a strategy

Union (YOON-yuhn)—the 23 states that remained loyal to the U.S. government during the Civil War

For Further Reading

Archer, Jules. *A House Divided: The Lives of Ulysses S. Grant and Robert E. Lee.* New York: Scholastic, 1995.

Clinton, Catherine. *Scholastic Encyclopedia of the Civil War.* New York: Scholastic Reference, 1999.

Collier, Christopher, and James Collier. *The Civil War, 1860–1866.* Drama of American History. New York: Benchmark Books, 1998.

Dosier, Susan. *Civil War Cooking: The Union.* Exploring History through Simple Recipes. Mankato, Minn.: Blue Earth Books, 2000.

Egger-Bovet, Howard, and Marlene Smith-Baranzini. *USKids History. Book of the American Civil War.* Brown Paper School. Boston: Little, Brown, 1998.

Graves, Kerry A. *Going to School during the Civil War: The Union.* Going to School in History. Mankato, Minn.: Blue Earth Books, 2002.

Green, Carl R., and William R. Sanford. *Union Generals of the Civil War.* Collective Biographies. Springfield, N.J.: Enslow, 1998.

Hakim, Joy. *War, Terrible War.* History of US. New York: Oxford University Press, 1999.

Places of Interest

Appomattox Court House National Historical Park
Highway 24
P.O. Box 218
Appomattox, VA 24522
http://www.nps.gov/apco
Where Lee surrendered
to Ulysses

General Grant National Memorial (Grant's Tomb)
Riverside Drive and 122nd Street
New York, New York
http://www.nps.gov/gegr
Tomb of Ulysses and Julia Grant

Grant Birthplace
1551 State Route 232
Point Pleasant, OH 45153
http://www.ohiohistory.org/places/grantbir
Ulysses's birth home

Mount McGregor Cottage State Historic Site
Wilton, NY 12831
Adirondack Mountains cottage where Ulysses wrote his memoirs and died

U. S. Grant Homestead
219 East Grant Avenue
Georgetown, OH 45121
Where Ulysses spent time growing up

U. S. Grant National Historic Site (White Haven)
7400 Grant Road
St. Louis, MO 63123
Federal park with historic buildings presenting the lives of Ulysses and Julia Grant

U.S. Military Academy
West Point, New York 10996
http://www.usma.edu/PublicAffairs/history
Items related to Ulysses, including a painting he did as a cadet; a statue in Cadet Chapel honors Ulysses and his oldest son, Frederick Dent Grant, also a West Point graduate.

Internet Sites

Do you want to learn more about Ulysses S. Grant?
Visit the FactHound at *www.facthound.com*

FactHound can track down many sites to help you. All the
FactHound sites are hand-selected by our editors. FactHound will
fetch the best, most accurate information to answer your questions.

IT'S EASY! IT'S FUN!
1) Go to *www.facthound.com*
2) Type in: **0736810919**
3) Click on **FETCH IT** and FactHound will put you on the trail
   of several helpful links.

You can also search by subject or book title. So, relax
and let our pal FactHound do the research for you!

Index